First Facts®

UNEXPLAINED MYSTERIES

The Unsolved Mystery of ALIEN ABDUCTIONS

by Michael Martin

CAPSTONE PRESS
a capstone imprint

First Facts are published by Capstone Press,
1710 Roe Crest Drive, North Mankato, Minnesota 56003
www.capstonepub.com

Library of Congress Cataloging-in-Publication Data
Cataloging-in-publication information is on file with the Library of Congress.
ISBN 978-1-4765-3095-6 (library binding)
ISBN 978-1-4765-3426-8 (eBook PDF)
ISBN 978-1-4765-3440-4 (paperback)

Editorial Credits
Anna Butzer, editor; Juliette Peters, designer; Wanda Winch, media researcher;
Kathy McColley, production specialist

Photo Credits
Corbis: Bettmann, 11, Dreamstime: Luca Oleastri, 21, Philcold, 18-19; Fortean Picture Library, 12; iStockphotos: Nathan Smith, 16; Mary Evans Picture Library: Michael Buhler, 15; Shutterstock: Fer Gregory, 4, Jennifer Gottschalk, fractal design element, Martin Capek, nebula design element, Mike Heywood, 8, Photobank.kiev.ua, 7, qcontrol, cover (UFO), razlomov, cover (alien), sgrigor, design element, zeber, design element

Printed in the United States of America in North Mankato, Minnesota.
032013   007223CGF13

Table of Contents

Chapter 1

Do Aliens Exist?

While driving home, Kelly and Andrew Cahill saw a large flying object. The Australian couple saw a bright flash a little later that August 1993 day. Then the sky was empty. Did they see an alien spaceship?

Once Kelly and Andrew got home, they discovered their trip took longer than usual. Kelly had nightmares about being in a spaceship. She said these nightmares helped her remember being **abducted** by aliens.

abduct—to take someone away by force

7

Chapter 2

History and Legend

Thousands of people have told stories about alien abductions. The first reports of alien abductions started in the 1950s. Many people believe the stories. **Skeptics** want more proof, such as metal from a spaceship or photos. Scientists are trying to solve the mystery of alien abductions.

skeptic—a person who questions things that other people believe in

One of the most well-known alien abduction stories was told by Betty and Barney Hill. The Hills were driving home September 19, 1961. They saw a bright light in the sky. They stopped to look at the object with **binoculars**. Barney saw that it looked like a spacecraft. When they got home, they realized their trip took longer than usual.

binoculars—a tool that makes far-away objects look closer

THE
INTERRUPTED
JOURNEY:
Two Lost Hours "Aboard a Flying Saucer"

by John G. Fuller

With an Introduction
by Benjamin Simon, M

Betty and Barney Hill

11

Two years later Barney and Betty were **hypnotized**. Barney remembered being on a spacecraft. Betty remembered creatures with gray skin and large eyes. The strange memories led Barney and Betty to report aliens had kidnapped them.

Memories of alien abductions are not always clear. People who believe they have been abducted are hypnotized several times. Sometimes many years pass before they can remember what happened.

hypnotize—to put another person into a sleeplike state; people sometimes recall memories better when hypnotized

Chapter 3

Studying Stories

Scientists and **researchers** have been studying alien abduction stories for the last 50 years. Budd Hopkins was a well-known researcher. He met with hundreds of people who believed they had been abducted. Hopkins hypnotized people to help them remember what had happened. Many people remembered events they could not explain.

researcher—someone who studies a subject to discover new information

Skeptics think books, TV shows, and magazines give people ideas about aliens. Many skeptics believe that people make up stories based on these ideas.

David Jacobs became curious about alien abductions after meeting Budd Hopkins. Jacobs is a retired history professor. He learned how to use hypnosis. He has hypnotized hundreds of people who have said they were abducted. Their stories were similar to stories that Hopkins had heard.

Some people believe aliens have the power to change the memories of people they have abducted.

True or False?

Does hypnosis help prove alien abduction stories are real?

True:
Many abductees who have been hypnotized have recalled hidden memories from their abductions.

False:
Not everyone believes in hypnotic research. Hypnosis can cause people to remember things that did not happen.

True:
Researchers say people seem really scared when they remember being abducted.

False:
Researchers say that it is easy to fake being scared.

Chapter 4

Searching for Answers

People who say they were abducted have little in common with one another. Some say they have seen aliens in the morning. Others say they have seen aliens at night. Some remember being abducted at home. Others say they were outside when they met aliens. These differences make studying alien abduction stories hard.

True or False?

Did a spaceship land in Great Britain's Rendlesham Forest?

True:
The U.S. Air Force had a base near the Rendlesham Forest in 1980. Several airmen reported seeing strange lights in the forest in December.

False:
The strange lights were later found to be from a nearby lighthouse. Investigators found that as the light turned, it flashed through the trees.

True:
Some men also said they saw a triangle-shaped metal object. Investigators saw three holes in the ground where the spaceship had been spotted. These holes formed a triangle.

False:
People who lived near the forest explained the three holes in the ground. They said they were rabbit burrows.

More people are beginning to wonder if aliens really visit Earth. Researchers look for **patterns** in the stories of abductees. They want to know if the thousands of stories from abductees are real. Maybe someday researchers will find the answers they are searching for.

pattern—several things that are repeated in the same way several times

21

Glossary

abduct (ab-DUKT)—to take someone away by force

binoculars (buh-NAH-kyuh-luhrz)—a tool that makes far-away objects look closer

hypnotize (HIP-nuh-tize)—to put another person into a sleeplike state; people sometimes recall memories better when hypnotized

pattern (PAT-urn)—several things that are repeated in the same way several times

researcher (REE-surch-ur)—someone who studies a subject to discover new information

retire (ri-TIRE)—to give up work, usually because of a person's age

skeptic (SKEP-tic)—a person who questions things that other people believe in

Read More

Polydoros, Lori. *Top 10 UFO and Alien Mysteries.* Top 10 Unexplained. North Mankato, Minn.: Capstone Press, 2012.

Walker, Kathryn. *Mysteries of UFOs.* Unsolved! New York: Crabtree Pub., 2009.

Wencel, Dave. *UFOs.* The Unexplained. Minneapolis: Bellwether Media, 2011.

Internet Sites

FactHound offers a safe, fun way to find Internet sites related to this book. All of the sites on FactHound have been researched by our staff.

Here's all you do:

Visit *www.facthound.com*

Type in this code: 9781476530956

Check out projects, games and lots more at
www.capstonekids.com

Index